SPEED
Cinema of Motion

The train clears the buffalo in *How The West Was Won* (1962).

SPEED
Cinema of Motion
by
Werner Adrian

Bounty Books

Copyright © MCMLXXV by Lorrimer Publishing Ltd.
Library of Congress Catalog Card Number: 75-37325 *3·20.6*
All rights reserved.
This edition is published by Bounty Books
a division of Crown Publishers, Inc.
by arrangement with Lorrimer Publishing Ltd.
a b c d e f g h
Manufactured in the United States of America

Designer: Dave Allen
Cover Designed by: JWA Designs Limited

CONTENTS

The publishers wish to thank the following organisations and people for their help in preparing this book:
The British Film Institute, 20th Century Fox, MGM-EMI, Columbia-Warner, United Artists, Allied Artists, Paramount, Universal MCA, RKO General Inc., Rank, First National, Cinema International Corporation, Hammer, the Cinema Bookshop, Anglo-Amalgamated, AIP, Contemporary Films, British Lion, Hemdale, Intercontinental Films, the stills and information departments of the National Film Archives, Titan International, Don Getz, Al Reuter, Brian McIlmail, Martin Jones, and United Press International.

THE MOVING PICTURE

The film is a moving picture. It depends on an optical illusion. If a camera takes twenty-four individual pictures each second and these pictures are projected on a screen at the same speed, the eye will see an illusion of human movement. It may be no more real than Plato's shadows on the wall, which we think may be life. For the cinema did begin as magic shadows. But through the principle of the wheel and the repeated image, these magic shadows became the moving pictures that we know today.

porary illustrations on the theme show. *(See Colour Section)* The cinema was also a medium of fantasy, as the early work of the magician Georges Méliès and his imitators such as Zecca demonstrate. Méliès constructed a studio to show special effects such as train crashes and voyages to the moon. And he found an audience in the fairgrounds that was used to staged trick-

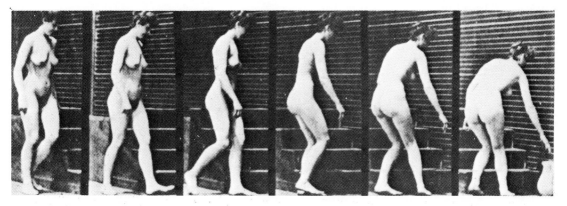

The American Muybridge in a series of famous photographic experiments beginning in 1872 managed to photograph humans and horses in motion.

The whirring wheels inside the camera and the projector found the whirling wheels of the train and the bicycle and the coach their favourite subjects, when the cinema was first invented in the 1890s. It was no coincidence that one of the first films made by the Lumière brothers in 1895 was the sequence of a train arriving at a station. Train effects were also dominant in early picture-books on the optical illusion of movement, such as 'The Motograph Moving Picture Book' of 1898, with its cover illustrated by Toulouse-Lautrec.

For early transportation was very much a fantasy of its time, as the wealth of contem-

effects and loved the obvious illusion of it all.

In fact, the early films were undercranked, which gave odd effects – carriage-wheels appeared to go backwards in motion when the films were projected at the proper speed. But generally, given the fact that the early camera was always fixed and the dolly and the mobile camera-head had not yet been invented, a pan shot was only possible if the camera itself was fixed to a moving object. Thus the earliest shots of moving pictures from a moving camera are taken from a gondola going down the Grand Canal in Venice and from an elevator going up the Eiffel Tower. Both of these sequences are taken from a slowly-moving object and thus do not suffer from the strobe effect

This early device, the electrical tachyscope of Ottomer Anschütz, showed a horse and rider apparently galloping. The inventor cranked a large wheel to give the illusion of motion.

Above: The traction engine appears to steam and move its wheel in The Motograph Moving Picture Book of 1898. *Right:* The train arrives in one of the first films of the Lumières.

A postcard montage view of 1910, showing how Paris would soon look.

The result of a Méliès crash.

Above: A man rides an aerial submarine in Zecca's film *La Machine Volante* (1905), while (*right*) lovers embrace under the sea in an early French postcard.

Below: **More early postcards show the fascination of early transportation.**

YOU ARE GOING TOO FAST IN MANCHESTER, N. H.

characteristic of the overhasty travelling shot.

What is evident in the early films is, the quicker that things moved towards the fixed camera, the more exciting it was for the audience. This explained the popularity of the onrushing train and early car and aeroplane. They were still strange objects to many country people, and their velocity still terrified many people in the towns. They were as weird to us as space-shots and flying saucers are today – the automobile of yesterday is the Star Trek of today. Transportation has moved its speed and myth from the near air, sea and earth to the farthest reaches of the heavens, where Mariner now probes at Mars.

It was no surprise that the first thriller made with intercut sequences in 1903 was called *The Great Train Robbery*. Edwin S. Porter used the device of bandits tying up a telegraph operator in order to rob a train undisturbed. Of course, the operator manages to wriggle free and tap out the morse code, so that the robbers are caught in the act. But communications are all. The cinema itself is another means of communication, of motion, of bringing messages from place to place, from people to people. It is part of the great revolution in connections that was to put a girdle round the earth in thirty seconds, quicker than any Puck.

For the twentieth century was to replace the train by the space-shot, the telegraph by the satellite, the hand camera by the world telecast. The invention of the recording of moving pictures was part of the great game of discovery in how to speed up the movement and responses and news of the world. *(See Colour Section)*

A French game shows the fascination of early invention.

The telegraph operator is forced by bandits to signal the train to stop in *The Great Train Robbery* (1903).

Forty years on, it was fun to see the same plot used in *Trapped By Wireless*, another thriller based on communications.

STEAM, RAIL AND IRON

The locomotive was the iron fist of progress in the nineteenth century. The railroad was the great civilizer and destroyer. If a wilderness was to be conquered, a continent to be crossed, the laying of the track was the first labour of the tens of thousands of Hercules, called navvies in England. In America, the locomotives could be the heroes, as in Buster Keaton's *The General*. They were certainly the metal messiahs of the new America in all the Western dramas about the railroad from *The Iron Horse* through *Union Pacific* to Leone's extraordinary hymn of praise to a period he only knew by imitation, *How the West Was Won*. There the shot of the engine charging and clearing the buffalo, the new machine against the ancient herd, is as significant as it is exciting. (Frontispiece)

The train was more than a method of getting from station to station in Victorian days. It was a dream of strength, a threat of disaster, a hope of liberation, a height of tension and of emotion. The cinema itself began with a documentary shot of a train coming into a French station. The magic of the train provoked the first model trick shot, when the English pioneer Paul filmed a railway collision in 1898. The ex-conjurer Méliès followed with his train smashes, although they always look as if they were staged, rather than simulated. But then Méliès remained determinedly unrealistic,

Buster Keaton examines his mighty engine in *The General* (1926) . . . and walks down the track, when he has lost it.

The train goes through in *Union Pacific* (1939).

A crash from a Méliès film

An early French 'baby' postcard, designed to encourage population growth.

far more in love with the magic world of the train, as shown in contemporary French postcards, than with the mere recording of the iron beast on its remorseless track.

What Paul and Méliès faked, early Hollywood did for real. The rise of stuntwork in films had much to do with the dangers of leaping onto trains, fighting on their roofs, or crashing them through obstacles. Although stars like Keaton and Fairbanks did their own stunts, the speed of the train and its risk to life and limb encouraged a new industry of doubles and stunt-workers. Many of these men were ex-daredevils or road-kids, used to riding the rods or jumping freights as hoboes. Twice the movies have dealt with this jungle world described by Jack London, once in the charming Louise Brooks film with Wallace Beery, *Beggars of Life,* where she dresses as a boy to ride the rods, and recently in the exciting Lee Marvin film, *Emperor of the North,* where the stars do fight to the death on the moving freight train.

The train as a dream of strength was really the invention of Abel Gance. His film of *La Roue* in 1921 made the engine a form of superego, charging down its determined track, adding resolution and even liberation through the will to human life, which had to be fought as a continual struggle for existence. Jean Renoir's *La Bête Humaine* of 1938 was strongest where Jean Gabin was the superman of the cab, the controller of the mighty engine of his own destiny. It was weakest where it used Zola's theories of heredity, making Gabin a pre-ordained epileptic killer due to his tainted blood, a kind of runaway engine down the metal tracks prejudged by his genes.

The station as the Smoky Valhalla of final parting in the movies is due both to literature and camera lighting. Some of the finest effects of chiaroscuro in black-and-white photographs have been created by the contrasts of smoke and steam against a night background. If Turner's painting of the Great Western called 'Rain, Steam and Speed', is probably the finest atmospheric painting of movement ever done, so the station sequence in *Alraune* of 1928 is one of the most evocative moments in the

Lee Marvin waits to jump the train in *Emperor of the North* (1973) . . . then he fights Borgnine to the death on the moving freight.

Gabin is driven to murder as certainly as the tracks conduct his train in *La Bête Humaine*.

Turner uses mist and steam in 'Rain, Steam and Speed'.

Steam from the engine also adds suspense to Hercule Poirot's appearance in *Murder on the Orient Express* (1974).

Marlene Dietrich is a creature of fantasy, seen through the blinds of *Shanghai Express* (1932).

An early French postcard catches the romance of Edwardian train travel . . . a romance rather lost in the recent *Murder on the Orient Express*.

German Expressionist Cinema, which concentrated obsessionally on the moods of the visual world of shadow and light.

Hollywood could also conjure up the wrenching melancholy of the smoky train most movingly in Greta Garbo's death in *Anna Karenina*, most mythically in Marlene Dietrich's performance as Lily in *Shanghai Express*. In that *tour de force* by von Sternberg, the corridors in the train are an excuse for the hallucinatory play of line and hazy light on a goddess of the cinema. Her compartment seems more enchanted than a boudoir of Scheherezade – certainly not a device for

The train is a passing joy and nostalgia in *Closely Observed Trains* (1966).

Edwin S. Porter's *The Great Train Robbery* of 1903 is . . . remade by John Wayne and others.

bundling a whole lot of stars together as in the modern *Murder on the Orient Express.* Of recent films, only the charming and nostalgic Czech *Closely Observed Trains* has caught the wonder and pleasure of the station in a town's life.

As a threat of disaster, the train may actually be the safest form of travel, but its collisions remain spectacular, as in de Mille's *The Greatest Show on Earth,* where not even the escape of the lions and elephants from the wrecked circus can stop the sawdust extravaganza going on next night. The blowing-up of trains with explosives has continued to provide major sequences of the cinema. In both of David Lean's major films, the derailing of the locomotive in *Lawrence of Arabia* and the ride of the armoured train through the tunnel and the snows in *Dr. Zhivago* are climaxes of the epic film. In Frankenheimer's *The Train,* the destruction of the iron beast is the cog of the plot; in fact, the actual filming of the train crash destroyed one camera. In Western after Western, the train is not only the symbol of progress and the new order,

The deadliest gold hunt of them all.

JOHN WAYNE
ANN-MARGRET
ROD TAYLOR
THE TRAIN ROBBERS

but also the moving palace of plunder and women. As the first American action picture of them all, with intercut sequences and a narrative, was called *The Great Train Robbery* and was a popular success, it is not surprising that the theme has been used again and again. Part of the attraction of the train seems to be the stark contrast of its luxury with the wilderness around. Both in *How*

The train is a palace on wheels to attack and plunder in Terence Young's *Red Sun* (1971).

the West Was Won and in *Red Sun,* the private railroad-car houses the corrupt and ruthless outsiders, who are attacked and destroyed by the purer savages with their horses of flesh-and-blood, and even samurai swords and code of honour.

The threat of disaster is not only in the train, but on the track. The tying of the victim to the sleepers in the path of the oncoming engine is a cliché of the serial and the cartoon. Yet even more murderous is the laying of the railroad track with its armies of convicts and desperate men

What can happen to Jerry at the hands of Tom . . . and (left) to Diana Rigg in *The Avengers*.

trying to survive the heat and the brutal conditions of survival. Mervin Le Roy's *I am a Fugitive from a Chain Gang* was both a harrowing exposure of prison conditions in the Southern States and one of the most heavily censored films ever to be mangled in Hollywood. In the coal-mines, the

Betty Hutton replayed the perils of the famous early serial queen.

Paul Muni toils on the railroad in *I Am A Fugitive from a Chain Gang* (1932).

Emlyn Williams checks out the coal mines in Carol Reed's *The Stars Look Down* (1939).

narrow track for the coal-tubs could also represent a life-destroying labour in the sweat and muck. It is the making of the track which kills thousands of British prisoners-of-war in *Bridge on the River Kwai*. It is the track which becomes the symbol of Nazi oppression in René Clement's *La Bataille du Rail* and has to be sabotaged by the Maquis. And it is the track which finally delivers the American prisoner Billy Pilgrim to the apocalyptic fire of Dresden in *Slaughterhouse Five*.

For the track is the parallel iron bars that crush human will and sever God's landscape. They deliver men as remorselessly as fate to their doom. If the laying of the track in de Mille's *Union Pacific* of 1939 can seem a message of human courage and hope, it is also the relentless coming tie by tie of the carriers of information and betrayal. The track itself, though, may be a liberator for those who labour to death on it. In *Cool Hand Luke*, Paul Newman escapes down the track, thus proving that all things can contain their own opposite, and that the chain can also become the flail of liberty. The incredible onrushing shots of the rails ahead, taken from the front of the locomotive in *La Bête Humaine* and *Night Mail*, also seem to make those iron lines as unrolling and liberating as that definition of infinity – the point where two parallel lines converge.

The ambiguity of the track also lies in the train. While Trotsky's armoured train can seem the symbol of liberation to the Communists, the sealed train in *We From Kronstadt* can appear to be the approaching symbol of oppression and disaster. While the train in the Western usually means the coming of capitalism and greed and exploitation in *How the West Was Won* or *The Treasure of Pancho Villa*, it may seem the platform of altruism in *Mr. Deeds Goes to Town*, that Capra hymn to the virtues of the New Deal of 1936. The coming of the train to displace the stagecoach can be applauded, as in one of Marilyn Monroe's minor films, *A Ticket to Tomahawk*. It can also be

The Maquis sabotage the track in René Clement's *La Bataille du Rail* (1944-45).

The old German commandant waits with his boy soldiers for the P.O.W.s in Dresden in *Slaughterhouse Five* (1972).

The labourers lay the track ahead of t locomotive in *Union Pacific*.

Cool Hand Luke (1967), played by Paul Newman, escapes down the track.

The locomotive is heavily defended in *How The West Was Won* . . . and heavily attacked in *The Treasure of Pancho Villa*.

Ann Baxter is astride by the train in *A Ticket to Tomahawk* (1950).

The train is the vehicle for generosity and small-town sense in Frank Capra's *Mr. Deeds Goes To Town* (1936).

the only hope of liberation, the last way out of town and death, as for Geraldine Chaplin in *Le Dernier Train* and Kirk Douglas in *Last Train from Gun Hill*. For the inevitable iron way into the trap is also the inevitable way out. The railroad rolls on, whether the hero buys his ticket or not.

Yet the trains which have provided the most terrifying sequences in film are the

King Kong destroys the EL in New York.

In *The Odessa File* (1974), the subway train is the wheels of approaching death.

An early French postcard showed the charm of the old tram . . . and Harold Lloyd plays its upper deck for laughs in *For Heaven's Sake* (1926).

elevated trains. The vision of the unknowing passengers in the El compartment hurtling towards their total destruction in the hands of the giant ape in *King Kong* remains a nightmarish vision of total catastrophe, which even the clever claustrophobia of the hijacked subway train in *The Taking of Pelham 1-2-3* cannot quite equal. Arguably, the best chase sequence ever shot is the pursuit of the killer under the elevated railroad by Gene Hackman in his automobile during *The French Connection*. The uncontrolled speed and ferocity of the train above, compared with the mad daring of the cop beneath, leads to a true climax as the killer is shot on the stairway of the high El station, as yet unequalled in thriller movies.

The tram on its tracks, however, has always seemed a vehicle for nostalgia or comedy. Harold Lloyd, of course, used it breathtakingly in *For Heaven's Sake*. Its

scale is human and its dangers always ridiculous. Equally farcical is the vision of the train which has left its tracks and careers about, unable to control itself. In one of the less amusing and more self-indulgent of the Ealing Comedies, an ancient train was made the hero; but in the last resort, *The Titfield Thunderbolt* could never equal the

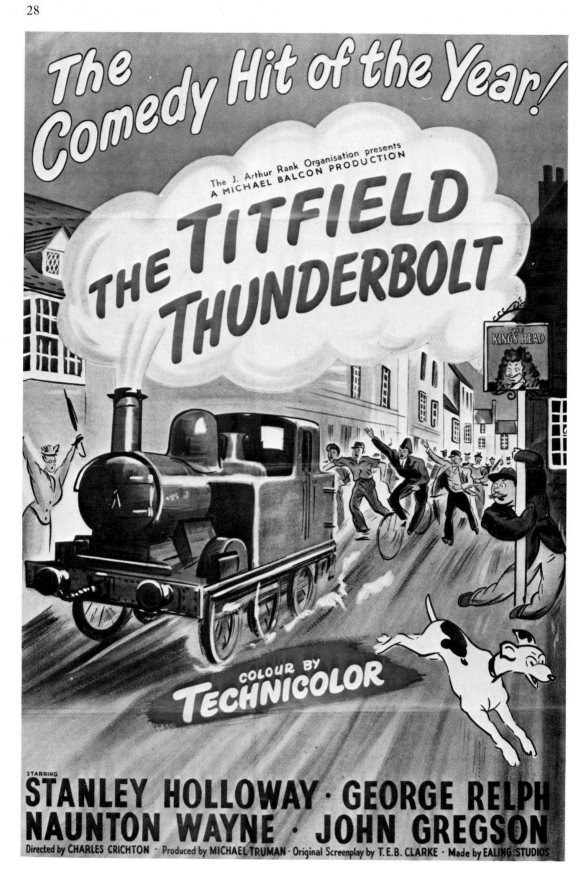

Will Hay plays the ticket-collector in the Ealing comedy, *Black Sheep of Whitehall* **(1941).**

In Arthur Penn's *Mickey One,* **the hero tries vainly to escape from the train.**

success of the earlier *Passport to Pimlico* or *Kind Hearts and Coronets.* Even a quaint locomotive was no substitute for Alec Guinness, and certainly not for Will Hay, playing the ticket collector.

So the train loses its qualities of dream and terror in a modern age which finds rail travel old-fashioned and space-shots the fact of today, not the fiction of science. The great American railroads are nearly bankrupt. They carry freight and have dropped passengers. Yet their mystique lives in the cinema. For they are above all the mighty engines of smoke and darkness, the screen symbols of mystery and power, the chosen brutes of progress, the carriers of hope and despair. We may try to forget them or escape them, but they remain implacable and remorseless in the camera eye.

SEA,UNDERSEA AND AIR

In a medieval parable, the air is the sea and the church steeples are anchors let down from heaven to stick on the earth's crust, so that God can fish for the souls of men. When the cinema began, sea voyages were old in human experience – too ordinary for much of a mystique. But voyages through the oceans of the atmosphere by airship (significantly so-called) and aeroplane, and voyages undersea by submarine, coincided with the experiments that invented the moving picture. If the first cinematic interest in transport went to the train, the second went to the new vehicles of the sky and the underwater. Only surface ships, outside sinking and storms, seemed too slow and rolling for the cinema of motion.

There were ship pictures, to be sure, where there had been a dramatic incident. Two expensive versions of the *Mutiny on the Bounty* were made, with the ship especially built for the film and the comfort of the stars. Sailing pictures about China clippers or whaleships such as *Windjammer* or *Moby Dick* or *Hawaii* could get a limited and repetitive action out of storms – but how often can the hero take over the wheel?

For every successful ship movie based on a best-selling novel such as *The Caine Mutiny*, there was a relative flop such as *Ship of Fools*. Unless there was an actual catastrophe to the liner as monumental and prolonged as the sinking of the Titanic in *A Night To Remember* or the topsy-turvy hull of *The Poseidon Adventure*, life on board a passenger

Even in *The Vikings,* the ship of the invaders is secondary on the poster to the stars.

This First World War postcard shows the new excitement about aircraft, while the old battleships are reduced in size smaller than the French soldier.

Brando at bay as the mutineer Fletcher Christian in the second version of *Mutiny on the Bounty* (1962).

George O'Brien takes over the ship's wheel in a storm in *Windjammer* (1930).

Humphrey Bogart plays Captain Queeg in *The Caine Mutiny* (1954).

Above right, and below: **When the ship foundered, there were some spectacular special effects in** *The Poseidon Adventure* **(1972).**

James Cagney and Frank McHugh polish the plugged guns of the American battleship in *Here Comes The Navy* (1934).

These two Russian posters of *The Battleship Potemkin* (1919) evidently make the ship the star of the film.

ship was really a less interesting *Grand Hotel* (unless the Marx Brothers were stowaways and reduced all orders to disorder). It is noticeable that such features as Hoot Gibson's *Out of Luck* or James Cagney's *Here Comes the Navy* put the sailors off-ship and on the town as often as scrubbing the deck or the guns. Even a battleship is a most restricted space for a film crew.

Of course, the first classic feature film of the Russian Revolution featured *The Battleship Potemkin*. It is the true star of the picture. We are taken through the social conditions that lead up to the revolt of the sailors and we end with the triumph of the *Potemkin* sailing unopposed through the other Russian ships sent in to attack it. Yet all the same, the climax of the picture takes place on land, when Czarist troops mow down the people on the Odessa steps. There is room on land for massacre and change of view and angle and level, for the movement of crowds and the tumbling ruin of the bodies. Only Douglas Fairbanks with his incredible agility and grace made a ship seem as full of acrobatic possibilities as an Arabian Palace in *The Black Pirate*, where his use of the swinging ropes and his

descent down a sail on the point of a knife gave the camera all the swooping freedom it can get from its unrestricted use.

It is significant that where there are hundreds of films about cavalry charges and aerial dogfights, there are hardly any about naval battles outside *Ben Hur*. Sea life and encounter simply do not have enough *motion* in them to interest the camera. In fact, the most successful of the ship movies outside the wartime propaganda vehicles such as *In Which We Serve* and *Convoy* and the recent sea-catastrophe

The ship dominates the men in *The Battleship Potemkin*.

36

In this 1961 cartoon version of Verne's tale, Captain Nemo's submarine is truly fantastic, more fish than metal.

In both *The Lost Continent* and *The Land That Time Forgot,* a world peopled by monsters is approached by life-boat and U-boat.

Monsters attack the U-boat in the ice in *The Land That Time Forgot* (1974).

pictures, starred a boat so small that it left room for the actors to win all eyes and hearts. It was the Bogart and Hepburn picture, *The African Queen*, where the muddy little riverboat of the title was the perfect foil to the inspired and loving bickering of the two stars. An old American cargo boat of no importance was also the understated background of John Ford and Mervyn Le Roy's *Mister Roberts*.

The crafts of the undersea are more interesting in their motion. They float forwards in a deep world of monsters. Their shapes are grotesque and mesmeric. Men cannot leave the trapped pockets of air within them without transforming themselves into rubber frogs or armoured divers. The underwater camera remains the recorder of an unseen and fantastic world for most of us, where the undulations of fish and squid are as phantasmagoric as our imaginings of mermaids. Jules Verne's undersea world of Captain Nemo has always seemed more real and possible – a lost Atlantis – than any prehistoric plateau of monsters discovered by balloon and camera. *(See Colour Section)*

While his father Daedalus stays close to the cool sea, Icarus flies too near to the sun.

Maris and Ki-Kung-Shi make their mythical flights.

A balloon did actually carry the first pioneer of the camera aloft in 1856, the extraordinary Nadar – here seen in Daumier's cartoon. The idea of flying gods and monsters was ancient – and certainly the idea of man flying was as old as the Greek legend of Icarus, who flew too close to the sun until the wax on his man-made wings melted in its heat. The Japanese wargod Maris rode a sacred flying boar, while the Chinese Prince Ki-Kung-Shi favoured a wind-driven aerial car. A miniature of 1320 showed the French king drawn through the air in a tent-chariot harnessed to griffins. Literal air-ships were

Griffins pull the French King through the air.

invented by later dreamers as vessels of the winds. In the year after the Montgolfier brothers actually ascended in a balloon, 1783, an aerial balloon-ship was launched into the air and sank to the ground like a wreck to the bottom. But balloons grew larger until they became the imaginary exploring craft of writers like Jules Verne,

In Walt Disney's *The Island at the Top of the World,* the explorers get into the gondola of an airship that looks just like a rail carriage . . . and land in disaster on the top of the world.

whose aerial ships inspired film-makers from Méliès to Walt Disney. *(See Colour Section)*

The early airships were actually floating vessels and the gondola swinging beneath them was like the cabin of a liner. In the First World War, the German Zeppelins delivered the first bombing raid on London, and barrage balloons on both sides did aerial and photographic reconnaissance from behind the front lines. But the airships proved vulnerable in war and liable to explosion in peace, as a whole series of actual dirigible disasters in the 1930s proved. Filmed versions of these flaming catastrophes came to the screen, but the

This drawing of the cabin of the Graf Zeppelin shows its size.

This early poster shows a stuntman using a gas balloon to get his man-kite up in the air.

giant floating ships of the air were too languid in motion to excite. Even so, the movie version of *Zeppelin* cost four technicians' lives to make.

The opposite was true of the early aeroplane, which was as jerky and jinking as an airborne polo pony. Although the first planes were themselves imitations, modelled more on box-kites than on birds, they immediately caught the attention of the public, and thus of the cinema. The early films knew the value of the unusual chase, and an aeroplane pursued a car in a Hepworth film soon after the invention of both machines. Yet it was the First World War again, which led to personal combats of the air, the dog-fights between the legendary Red Baron Richthofen's Flying Circus and the Allied squadrons. From the epic *Wings* of 1929, Hollywood made a succession of extraordinary aerial films, because of the superhuman courage of the pilots and stuntmen who worked for them. After *Wings* came *The Dawn Patrol, The Sky Hawk, Hell's Angels, Hell Divers, The Lost Squadron, Night Flight, Devil Dogs of the Air, China Clipper,* and *Test Pilot.* Although these films starred Humphrey Bogart and James Cagney in similar tough pilot roles, none of them captured the mystique of flying through the trackless ocean of the night. His failure to play with depth and meaning

Stuntman Gene Perkins was killed by this stunt.

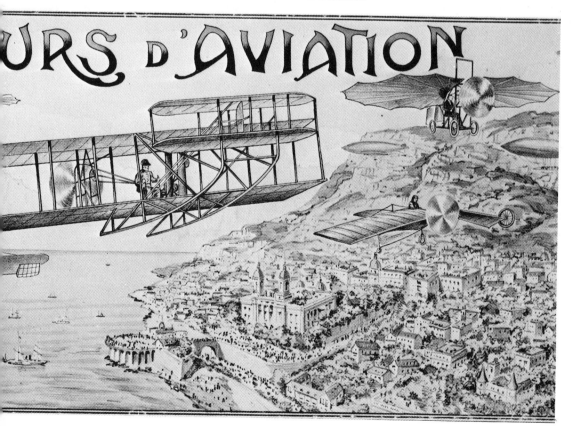

More stuntmen died in the making of *Wings,* from which this still comes.

James Cagney plays the tough pilot in *Devil Dogs of the Air* (1935).

A scene from *The Dawn Patrol* (1930).

Clark Gable also plays the tough pilot and survivor of a plane crash in many flying roles.

Jean Harlow favours the brave survivors in *Hell's Angels* (1927-30).

Saint-Exupéry's hero in *Night Flight* was the most conspicuous mistake in Gable's career. None of these films again equalled the sadness and terror of the last sequence in *King Kong*, when the melancholy giant ape swats the killing fighter-planes as if they were more contemptible than pterodactyls before falling to his uncomprehending death.

Yet, however ordinary the scenarios and direction of these early Hollywood chronicles of the pioneers of the air, the stunt pilots and planes were the heroes and brought in the audiences. Working on *Hell's Angels*, three stunt pilots were killed and many others injured. Sometimes the Californian sky seemed as dangerous as that of Flanders in 1917. When later the cinema came back to reconstruct the dogfights of those early days, the risks were still as appalling. *The Blue Max* and *The Red Baron* were both marked with injury and

The German machine flies upside down in *Those Magnificent Men in their Flying Machines*.

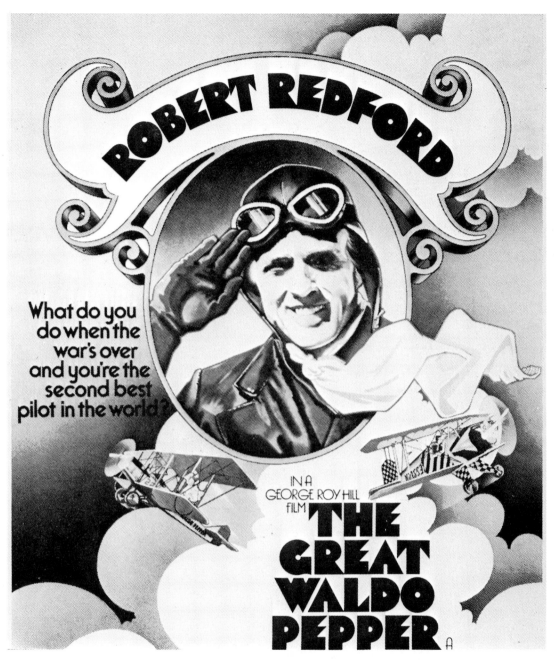

fatality. The luckiest and funniest reconstruction of those pioneer days of aviation, *Those Magnificent Men in their Flying Machines,* created the most superb stunt shots ever filmed and was a hilarious testament to the first lunatics who believed that their incredible constructions might actually voyage through the air. The most recent high jinks of praise to the early barn-stormers and stuntmen of space, Robert Redford's *The*

Great Waldo Pepper, has marvellous aerobatics and daring-do, but it does not capture either the profound feeling of uselessness of the retired First World War pilots or the occasional lyrical forgetful moments of the high air. *(See Colour Section)*

The hopelessness of the drunken exflyers was captured by William Dieterle in his little-known masterpiece on the debris of the First World War, *The Last Flight* of

Stunts and crashes galore in *The Great Waldo Pepper*.

Marlene Dietrich in leather flying-suit with Victor McLaglen in *Dishonoured* (1931).

1931. His scriptwriter was John Saunders, who took the story from his own novel 'Single Lady'. Four pilots sit around in Paris, drinking themselves to death in 1918 and revolving round a mutual and hopeless love for a girl called Nikki, played by Helen Chandler. Alcohol in the bloodstream is their substitute for adrenalin in the high cockpit and death at the end of the propellor. Most of their buddies are dead; they do not know why they survive. They do exactly what they say they will do in the opening dialogue of the film:

   – Well, the old guerre is finie.
   – That's right.
   – What you going to do now?
   – Get tight.
   – Then what?
   – Stay tight.

The fantasy of flight in the thirties was captured best by a mythological actress such as Dietrich or a futurist aeroplane, such as Cabal's in *Things to Come,* or a landing in a

John Cabal arrives in *Things To Come* (1935).

lost paradise such as Shangri-La. In her spy pilot's role in *Dishonoured,* Marlene Dietrich plays for ten minutes with a revolver and a black leather flying suit in the most equivocal and masculine sequence in her career.

She looks far more formidable than Cabal arriving in his black outfit to engineer the future of the world. There was nothing

Maureen O'Sullivan sits in her cockpit above the imaginary New York of 1980 in *Just Imagine* **(1930).**

The air passengers pass out . . . then revive in Shangri-La in the first version of Frank Capra's *Lost Horizon* **(1972).**

silly or romantic about Dietrich as a pilot in the way there was when Maureen O'Sullivan sat in a cockpit above New York, 1980, in America's response to the futurist *Metropolis* – the unsuccessful *Just Imagine* of 1930. Dietrich dominated anything she did, especially when her clothes suited her magisterial looks. She was as remote and dream-like as any beauty of the Shangri-La reached by the aeroplane travellers in *Lost Horizon*.

Curiously enough, the best film about the psychology of a pilot hardly showed an aeroplane at all. Jean Renoir's *La Regle du Jeu* has as its hero André Jurieu, who has just flown the Atlantic single-handed like the fêted Lindbergh. While the actual film about Lindbergh, Warner's *The Spirit of St Louis* with James Stewart playing the hero, failed to capture the wonders and terrors of the solitary flight despite interminable flying time, Renoir showed in his sequence of Jurieu's arrival in France the sheer inconsequence of a brave action. Jurieu scandalises everyone by asking after his

Jurieu doesn't give a damn for bravery when he arrives after his transatlantic journey in Renoir's *The Rules of the Game* (1939).

mistress, ignoring the great French public and what he has done. Later, out at the house-party at the chateau which is the core of the film, Jurieu fails to run away with his mistress because he is bound by a code of masculine honour as careful as a log-book. When he is killed by the game-keeper by mistake, his death for nothing is as true as his survival of the publicised dangers of the

Ground control is pretty pleased with Michael Redgrave's bombing efforts up above in *Way To The Stars* (1945).

flight. For there are no rules in the game of life and death and survival. There is only notoriety. To die in the cockpit of a winged machine is the same bloody useless waste as to die in an arm-chair by the fire. Dead. Dead. Dead. Dead. Dead.

The Second World War spawned a blitz of aeroplane movies that owed far more to propaganda than entertainment. Britain's *Way to The Stars* and *Target for Tonight* were full of the quiet heroism of the bombing crews who set out to destroy Germany, while the American *Flying Tigers* was a swash-buckling effort to praise their mercenary pilots for Chiang-kai-Shek.

THE
J. ARTHUR RANK
ORGANISATION
presents

FASTER THAN SOUND come
the sensational thrills in this
modern epic of the air......

THE NET

STARRING
PHYLLIS CALVERT
JAMES DONALD
ROBERT BEATTY
HERBERT LOM
WITH **MURIEL PAVLOW**

Screenplay by
WILLIAM FAIRCHILD
Directed by
ANTHONY ASQUITH

KENNETH MORE —

REACH FOR THE SKY

The Story of DOUGLAS BADER

MURIEL PAVLOW · LYNDON BROOK
LEE PATTERSON · ALEXANDER KNOX

After the war, the congratulatory self-praise by the British cinema of the exploits of the Royal Air Force and the plane makers reached an apogee with *Malta Story, Reach for the Sky* about the legless flyer Bader, played by Kenneth More, and other movies about the inventors of the Spitfire and the jet engine. There was even a thriller called *The Net* about breaking through the sound barrier. But when the blitz picture to end all air pictures was made, *Battle of Britain,* it was already shot too late. By the end of the sixties, the fashion for heroism and war nostalgia was waning. Europe had to be scoured to find enough old planes to limp

The Luftwaffe prepares to take off . . . It blasts the British airfields but the Spitfires came back in *Battle of Britain* (1969).

Abbott and Costello get up to aerial high jinks.

into the skies again. And impressive as the recreation of the old combats was, the heart had gone out of the matter, and Britain's Finest Hour had already become something of a museum piece.

American air-war films were more ironic, although they did not usually become as ribald as Abbott and Costello in *Keep 'Em Flying*. William Wyler's *The Best Years of our Lives* of 1946 was the only one influenced by the British cinema in its understated praise of bombers and the men who flew them. Other air pictures such as *Above and Beyond* and *The Bridges at Toko-Ri* were far more gung-ho because of the Korean war. Rarer was the reaction from war shown in the savage sequences of the Japanese air attack on Pearl Harbour in *From Here to Eternity*. Following up this attitude in *Catch-22,* Mike Nichols made the departure of the bombers on a raid look like a convoy of pregnant ducks labouring aloft in a heat wave, while

The American bomber crews fly off in *Above and Beyond* (1952).

The American attackers get a hard time at *The Bridges at Toko-Ri* (1954).

The Japanese fighters attack in *From Here To Eternity* (1953).

In *Catch-22,* the bombing missions seem both farcical and horrible.

the cockpit was more the home for horrors and hosing out corpses than for heroics. The film was so sickeningly anti-war that it ended by nearly sickening the audiences. And it found no pleasure in flight. In the terminal bombers, indeed, of *Dr. Strangelove* and *Fail Safe,* all human destruction lies in the atomic bombs under their wings.

For the terror and the beauty of men flying has remained to haunt the screen and move with the moving picture. Who can ever forget the chase of Cary Grant by the killer crop-dusting plane in *North by North-West?* Equally horrible was the slow hunt of fugitives by helicopter, remorselessly in *Figures in a Landscape,* commonly in a hundred other thrillers. Occasionally the fugitive fights back against the hovering mechanical harpy that hunts him like the evil mythical agents of the gods; but it takes a Tarzan to bring it down. The giant whirly-

THE MOST EXPLOSIVE STORY OF OUR TIME!

FAIL SAFE

Cary Grant tries to flee the pursuing plane in Hitchcock's *North-by-North-West* (1959).

SEE TARZAN AS YOU HAVE NEVER SEEN HIM BEFORE CHALLENGING THE WORLD'S MOST MODERN WEAPONS!

ANGLO AMALGAMATED presents
THE
SY WEINTRAUB PRODUCTION of
TARZAN
AND THE
VALLEY of GOLD 'U'
in PANAVISION and
EASTMAN COLOUR

birds nearly always win like Puff, the Magic Dragon which flew over Vietnam whispering the taped voices of the Viet Cong like ghosts in the night, demanding surrender; it could also so shoot up one of God's half-acres with programmed machine-gun bullets that no living thing could survive. Faced with such aerial monsters, how can the cinema ignore the new terror of death from the sky?

Speed is the essence of the moving picture, and the flying creatures of the air have speed. In the old days, it may have taken *13 Hours By Air* from New York to San Francisco, but now it is five hours by Boeing, although much the same dramas aloft are played by Charlton Heston and Raquel Welch in *Airport, '75* as by Fred MacMurray and Joan Bennett on the slower plane. For a cabin in space is a cabin in space is a cabin in space, and fear of a crash is all. The menace of man's flight is as powerful as its grace. It is both a destruction and a liberation, a horror and a happy dream.

The helicopters menace in *Billion-Dollar Brain* and in *Caravan to Vaccares*.

A spare pilot is dropped down by helicopter to help Raquel Welch pilot the stricken plane in *Airport '75*.

This early version of plane drama plays on our fears of claustrophobia aloft.

The aeroplane is a dream of liberation for the two young lovers in Antonioni's *Zabriskie Point* of 1970.

The plane is a fantasy photograph in *Closely Watched Trains* . . . worthy of the early romantic days of transport in France.

BIKE

An early French drawing of the new bicyclist by Hap.

When the bicycle was invented at the turn of the century, it seemed to adults what today it seems to children. It was escape, liberation, happiness, even speed. In H. G. Wells's novel, 'Mr. Polly', the bicycle is the triumph of the clerk and the shopkeeper. It goes as fast as the rider wishes. It does not depend on petrol or a machine that can go wrong. It is silent and free-wheeling, far from the factory, more reliable than the new car. (See Colour Section) The bicycle is for the individual and for love.

The French, who have always hallowed the bicycle in their famous race, the Tour de France, have always championed the bicycle in the cinema. It is the means of escape for the convict-boss in *A Nous la Liberté* by René Clair. It is the workers' tool and freedom in *Le Jour Se Lève* by Marcel Carné. If no French actor has ever equalled the hilarious solemnity on a high bicycle of Harry Langdon in *Long Pants* or of Bob Hope in *Never Say Die*, the bicycle remains a lyric break-out from convention, a free-wheeling into joy – best caught in the most romantic of sequences in the American success, *Butch Cassidy and the Sundance Kid*, when Paul Newman spins along to the music of a pop song, and the final shot is of the fallen spokes of the bicycle-wheel glittering with drops of water like salt diamonds in the sun.

Just as the battleship launched a classic film after the First World War in *Potemkin*, so the bicycle sent off another classic film in Italy after the Second World War, *Bicycle Thieves*. In De Sica's masterpiece of neo-realism, the hero's job and family depend on his bicycle. When it is stolen, he has lost everything, and his search for his bicycle becomes a desperate quest for survival. De Sica's skill is in using the little object of the bicycle as the symbol of the despair, poverty and unemployment of post-war Italy. The fact that it is the difference between life and a slow death gives the small scale of the film its universal meaning.

Yet the significance and romance of the bicycle gave way to the menace of the motorbike. The rise of the bike gangs of the 1950s was a social phenomenon, reflected in the cinema and spread by it. Marlon Brando

Bob Hope eyes Martha Raye in *Never Say Die* (1939).

in *The Wild One* of 1953 alone founded a cult for the motorbike and a pattern of violent behaviour that has never left our roads nor our screens. From the first time that he rode in with his bike gang to terrorize the small town, he outraged censors and scared older people in many of the countries of the world, where the film was banned. He represented savagery and anarchy, an attack on all the values of property and morality. It was best summed-up in his famous reply to the question of the girl in the cafe:

– What are you against?
– What have you got? Brando said.

Thus Brando and director Lazlo Benedek spawned the motorbike movie of violence and terror. He had many imitators, growing

The bicycle is bought, enjoyed and lost in de Sica's *Bicycle Thieves* (1947).

more and more full of brutality and rape and death. There was an escalation between *The Wild One* and Roger Corman's *The Wild Angels* of 1966 that seemed to glorify the notorious Hell's Angels of California, the most publicised of the West Coast bike gangs. The lead was played by the young Peter Fonda, whose previous screen appearance on a motorbike had been in the charming *The Young Lovers*. Now he played Heavenly Blues, leading his thugs in a Nazi orgy in a church, the vandalising of a town, and a curious bike funeral with a ritual as precise as a proper hearse to a cemetery. Corman gave the whole film the look of a documentary – and scored a hit with the tens of millions of motorbike-mad kids across the world.

The gang, led by Brando, come into town to terrorise it in *The Wild One*.

A BIG CHROME BABY and a BLACK LEATHER DOLL ...both Hotter, Faster, Tougher than most men can handle.

BURWALT PRODUCTIONS Presents

THE HARD RIDE

Two French fantasies of 1900 about the future of transportation.

A poster of 1896 about the stage success, *The Great Train Robbery,* which Edwin S. Porter was to make into the first action film in 1903.

FROM THE AUTHOR OF 'TARZAN

THE LAND THAT TIME FORGOT

CAMPAIGN BOOK CAST · CREDITS · STORY · BIOGRAPHIES · COMPETITIONS
NEWSPAPER SERIALISATION · POSTERS · PRESS BLOCKS · ACCESSORIES

A modern fantasy of discovering a lost world of prehistoric monsters by submarine —
The Land That Time Forgot.

Jules Verne is invoked for the domination of the human race by airship in *Master of the World*.

Robert Redford was the star in the recent nostalgic film on the early stunt fliers — *The Great Waldo Pepper*.

A French advertisement of 1910 thinks the bicycle is superior to the early car.

In the James Bond movie, *You Only Live Twice,* fantasies of transportation have made a great leap skyward.

CHUCK BERRY · LITTLE RICHARD · JERRY LEE LEWIS · BO DIDDLEY

KEEP ON ROCKIN'

A FILM BY D. A. PENNEBAKER

Produced and Released By Pennebaker

Pennebaker's *Keep on Rockin'* adds music to the cult of the motorbike.

In Corman's *Big Bad Mama*, the car is the women's chariot of death.

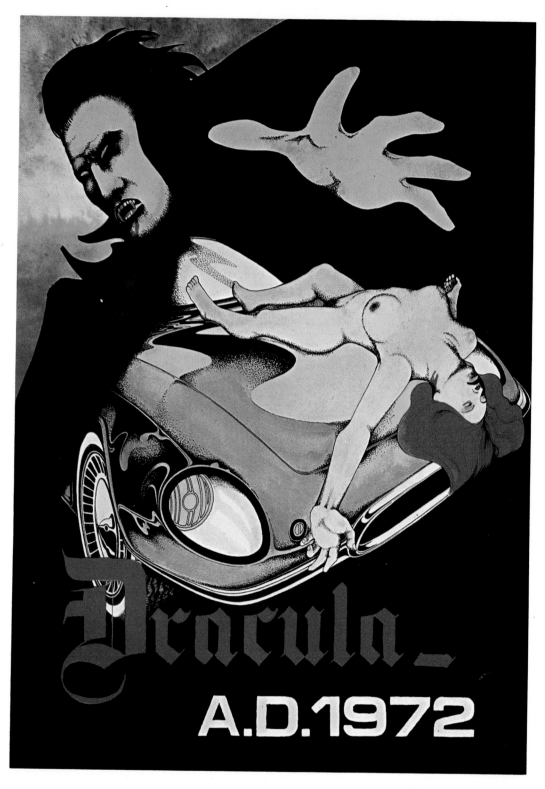

The Hammer poster for *Dracula A.D. 1972* puts vampires, sex and cars in a mixture of ancient myth and the modern cult for speed.

The grand finale of human dreams of reaching the furthest stars is seen in Kubrick's masterpiece *2001*.

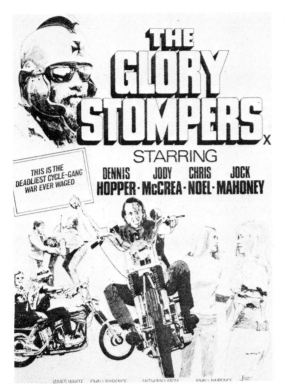

This death-rider comes from the American production of *Tales from the Crypt* (1973).

Hopper, Fonda and Nicholson take to the road in *Easy Rider*.

For the motorbike with its power and speed added a dimension of aggression to the liberty brought by the bicycle. There was a mystique in the protective clothing needed for the motorbike – goggles, gauntlets, jackets, boots – that fed on those people who loved the gear of authority and domination. At one extreme, films like *The Glory Stompers* of 1968 or *Hell's Angels '69* or *The Hard Ride* or *Angels From Hell* merely seem to be trying to glorify the gangs and advocate an all-out war on society. At another extreme, the motorbike becomes the symbol of death, the two-wheeled horseman of the apocalypse, with gangs of the undead riding their bikes up from under the earth, or skeleton riders burning through the night on their missions of revenge. As the ultimate of all these exploitation motorbike movies advertised:

A MACABRE STORY OF TWO MOTORCYCLE RIDING, KNIFE-WIELDING, AXE-SWINGING, SCALPEL-FLASHING, ACID-THROWING, GUN-SHOOTING, CHAIN-LASHING, ARM-TWISTING, BONE-BREAKING, NECK-WRINGING, SHIV-SHOVING, EYE-GOUGING, PATHOLOGICAL NUTS AND THEIR PAL— *THE UNDERTAKER.*

Yet because of its image of alienation and aggression, the motorbike became the symbol of the lone star and supermale of the 1960s. Where Brando led, Steve McQueen and Peter Fonda followed. McQueen actually did some extraordinary motorbike stunts in *The Great Escape* (1963) and was a drag racer. Fonda, of course, made the most successful of all bike pictures with Dennis Hopper, *Easy Rider.* Its triumph in 1969 changed the emphasis of motorbike pictures from berserk violence to praise of the bikers as lyric outlaws. *Easy Rider* restored the magic of the early bicycle to the late chopper. The first half of the film is an odyssey across the American West, full of sun-shots and refracted lenses, cool in the wind of their speed. A new style of movie-making emerges with the rambling appearance of Jack Nicholson, telling a space story and holding the film by his charm and manner as wholly as Michel Simon did, playing the tramp in *L'Atalante.* The film only fails in the New Orleans sequences, where the motorbikes are ditched for a second-rate psychedelic trip. But the aimless amoral tragedy of the end makes the Easy Riders the victims of society, not its

The aimless killing of Hopper ends *Easy Rider,* with Peter Fonda kneeling by his body.

The artist in the gorilla-suit breaks away in Reisz's *Morgan* (1966).

aggressors. So the bully becomes the scape-goat, and the motorbike is changed by Fonda from assault vehicle to freedom wheel.

There had been intimations of this change before, particularly in the remarkable sequence in Karel Reisz's *Morgan – A Suitable Case For Treatment*, when David Warner speeds in his smoking gorilla-suit towards the Thames. Warner represents the crazy liberated hero, as does Joe Namath in *C. C. and Company,* which set Namath *against* the gang, and the far more interesting *Hex,* which is the first 'nostalgia' motorbike movie. In it, a gang led by Keith Carradine come on their motorbikes in 1919 to a Nebraska farm, where two sisters are living who have supernatural powers through Indian ancestors. One sister uses Indian spells to destroy most of the gang, but the

Keith Carradine with sidecar passenger in *Hex* (1974).

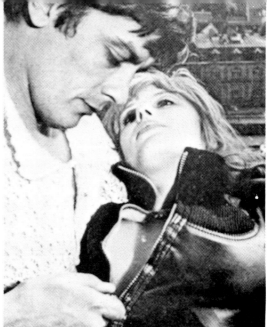

Alain Delon makes love to Marianne Faithfull in *Girl on a Motorcycle* (1967).

old bikes with their side-cars on the way to California are more spell-binding than even the avenging owls.

The motorbike also became a sex-object, used by advertising men and film-makers as a symbol of male power, on which a naked girl should ride. One feature in particular used this theme as its whole plot, the remarkable *Girl on a Motorcycle* made by Jack Cardiff and starring Alain Delon and Marianne Faithfull. The film is entirely about the long death rides of Marianne Faithfull, wearing a black leather suit lined with white fur, as she speeds from her husband's bed to a rendez-vous with her lover. Along the road, she has her erotic fantasies in which he slowly strips her of her leather suit; she also is a bareback rider in a circus-ring. Yet fate is waiting for her and she is killed just before her assignation.

With the public reaction from the youth-and-freedom movies of the late 1960s to the law-and-order movies of the mid-1970s, the motorbicycle became the instrument of enforcement. The speed cop took over as hero from the easy rider. In *Magnum Force*, Harry manages to escape on one of the bikes of the cops, which ends by bringing him down, as does Bronson in *The Mechanic*. Yet the most interesting and ambiguous of all the speed cop movies was *Electra Glide in Blue*, where Robert Blake playing Winter-green is forced to gun down his friend Zipper Davis, who began by persecuting a

gang of hippy bike-riders and ended by joining them.

The values of *Electra Glide in Blue* contain without discrimination nearly all the mythology of bicycle and motorbike – escape to the wilderness, individual choice, authority against freedom, the cult of the uniform, sudden violence, and the strange peace of the long trip on the road to somewhere, to nowhere, as long as the wheels are moving.

Clint Eastwood takes a fall in *Magnum Force* (1973).

Batman turns the motorbike into the greatest escape fantasy of all.

SADDLE, COACH AND CAR

The inland sea of the steppe and the desert and the prairie was the ground for the great cavalry of the world – the Mongols and the Arab horsemen and the mounted Indians and cowboys. While the hordes of Genghis Khan have never provided great cinema, the exploits of Lawrence of Arabia and the Young Churchill have filled the screen with stunts from the saddle just as successfully as innumerable Westerns. *(See Colour Section)* Yet the place where the horses gallop dominates their use. Without the flat, they cannot reach their full speed and beauty. Thus they are the creatures of their landscape, which can often reduce them to the size of beetles in a sand-pit.

Outside the gee-gee comedies, such as *The Lady's From Kentucky* and the children's epics, such as *Black Beauty* and *My Friend Flicka*, the horse has never dominated a picture as a battleship does in *Potemkin*, the bicycle in *Bicycle Thieves*, or even the vehicle in *Stage-coach*. The reason is that the horse on its own is really a creature of sentiment – except in that wonderful short film to liberty, *Crin Blanc*, where the white stallion of the Camargue escapes his pursuers to the sea. Many an action picture can climax in a cavalry charge, which allows both the rush of the momentum of the massed riders and the individual stunts of tripping and falling; but where the charge is the *only* point of the

John Wayne dominates in Ford's *Horse Soldiers* (1959).

Genghis Khan menaces Saxon children in Lang's *Kriemhild's Revenge* (1924).

What are horses to the desert even in *Stagecoach*?

PARAMOUNT'S
PULSE - POUNDING
RACING ROMANCE !

THE LADY'S FROM KENTUCKY

The slow-motion charge in de Laurentis version of *Waterloo* was effective, but the horses were still unable to salvage the movie, despite Christopher Plummer's playing of Wellington to Rod Steiger's neurotic Napoleon.

Douglas Fairbanks mounted in *The Iron Mask* (1929).

movie, as in *The Charge of the Light Brigade* or in the innumerable versions of Custer's Last Stand, the films are rarely successful. Where the horsemanship is incidental, as in Douglas Fairbanks' *The Iron Mask* or even in Laurence Olivier's *Henry V*, it can be a moving part of a successful film. But the horse on its own can no longer carry the audience as it once did the shock troops of medieval war.

In historical movies, of course, the horse – particularly when yoked to the chariot – can provide some of the dash and vigour that is the vision of the camera. In both the versions of *Ben-Hur*, the chariot-race is a real and dangerous climax to the picture. The plot sets up the race as an individual battle-to-the-death between hero and villain, and thus gives it the true urgency which makes for the success of the epic picture. Yet once again the horse is secondary to the people, to the plot. Even in the Western, the horse does not dominate in the

Laurence Olivier prepares for Agincourt in *Henry V* (1944).

The mounted Kirk Douglas leads the slave revolt against the Roman Legions in *Spartacus* (1960).

The film car shoots the chariots in the early version of *Ben-Hur* (1959-60).

Harpo Marx has the last word on chariot races in *Horse Feathers* (1932).

The cavalry fights in *Soldier Blue* are aimless.

age of the mass worship of the car and the gun and sex. We may have known the name of Gene Autrey's horse, but it is the naked Indian girl who looms in the foreground of the distant US cavalry in the poster of *Soldier Blue*, while the horse is secondary to the brutality of the film.

It is the girl in the wagon which upstages the horse in *Wagonmaster*, the gun at the hip or in the hand that dominates horseback riders or the buggy. Occasionally, as in *Duel in the Sun*, the horse is properly used as an economic symbol of the free range resisting the advance of settled farming and barbed wire – then it is given the dominant

role, not men. Yet in general, it has been reduced to a secondary, if not sentimental, role behind its main actors – the servant of its masters on the screen. Even Steve McQueen in his rodeo picture *Junior Bonner* steals the picture from the bronco.

Not so with a stagecoach, which has always had a symbolism beyond its use. It has ever been the hearse, the carrier of death from the early Méliès movies through Sjostrom's *The Phantom Carriage* of 1920 and René Clair's surrealistic *Le Voyage Imaginaire* and *Entr'acte* of 1925. In *Boul' de Suif*, it is the vehicle of social hypocrisy which delivers the French passengers and the

In *A Duel in the Sun* (1946), the horse plays its proper role in Western history.

The coach is a vehicle for love and style in the Fred Astaire and Ginger Rogers film, *Top Hat* (1935).

The coach is still stylish, but more ominous in Max Ophuls' *Madame de . . .* (1952).

prostitute to the Germans to expose *bourgeois* nastiness. It is the vehicle of style and romance in *Top Hat* and in Max Ophuls' *Madame de . . .* In *Stagecoach* of 1939, the plot revolves around the coach getting through Indian territory, and it becomes the force of civilisation against savagery, of bravery against treachery. It passes deserts, crosses rivers, provokes the battle between cavalry and Indians. The sequence of the uncoupling of the tongue between the lead

The perils of *Stagecoach*.

The stage represents civilization . . . and the need to defend it.

An early French postcard, when the car was still an open coach.

horses made a legend out of the stuntman Yakima Canutt. It was such a dangerous stunt that Ford decided he would never shoot such a sequence again. But it had been recorded and *Stagecoach* became the classic Western of all time.

In the way that the first makers of car bodies were called carriage-builders, and the bus in England is still called a coach, the first motorcars were still seen as horse-powered, rather than horse-drawn, vehicles. They were little faster than bicycles, and far more prone to disaster. Early drivers travelled hopefully and often did not arrive. Certainly the train was a far surer and quieter method of travel.

Thus the automobile in early days of the cinema was an object of farce, not of mass fantasy. In the Mack Sennett comedies, the Tin Lizzie and the Fire Engine were the rushing excuses for pratfalls at high speed. All the great early comics used the automobile as a literal comedy vehicle, from Harold Lloyd in *Hot Water* to Buster Keaton to Laurel and Hardy in most of their films. The motorcar was a sneaky inanimate vehicle with a will of its own, liable to drop

Harold Lloyd gives up between car and tram and family in *Hot Water* (1924).

to pieces around the driver and career along out of control. If its innards were not quite as baffling as they seemed to Bull Montana in *The Lost World*, yet they could play the most terrible tricks on the drivers. The zaniness of the comic car sequence probably reached its hilarious prolonged climax in

Stan Laurel and Oliver Hardy give up in *Air Raid Wardens* (1943).

Bull Montana is puzzled in *The Lost World* (1925).

the finale of W. C. Fields' *Never Give a Sucker an Even Break*, when Fields is rushing a woman he wrongly believes to be pregnant to hospital. He ends up, of course, carrying only the steering-wheel of his collapsed car. Even Doris Day managed to be hilarious in a car wash, where the roof suddenly opened up on her in *Move Over, Darling*. The car was an endless comic possibility.

The early automobile soon developed into a symbol of elegance. Norma Talmadge stepped in and out of it, as into a royal carriage. It was the devil-coach of Adolphe Menjou in *The Sorrows of Satan* and it became the gleaming introduction of Jean Harlow, when she was first discovered in a Hal Roach comedy of 1928. The great open touring cars were the symbol of the flappers and junkets of the time in *The Jazz Age* of 1927, as they raced down the roads from speakeasy to crash and *Dinner at the Ritz*. Even when the tourer became the symbol of destruction and remorse as in de

Above: W. C. Fields still at the wheel.

Below: Jean Harlow with Laurel and Hardy tends to upstage her vehicle in *Double Whoopee* (1928).

Left: Norma Talmadge's car is like a royal coach.

82

Easy riders from *The Jazz Age* (1927).

Mille's early film *Manslaughter*, the iron beast was more glamorous than threatening. In France, the car even began to acquire something of the status of the train as a myth in early serials and photographs, particularly in Feuillade's legendary *Judex* of 1916 and in one remarkable photograph taken in the Bois de Boulogne in 1925, where the *demoiselles* of the wood seem to be stepping into a black coach of sin which will take them anywhere.

By the time of the Great Crash and the thrillers of the 1930s, the car had taken upon itself much of the glamour of the cult of speed. It was the chariot of the gangster; with its spitting sub-machine guns, it was the armoured train of the mob; it was the

A slight dent in *Dinner at the Ritz*.

83

The speed cop dies on the fast lady's bonnet in de Mille's *Manslaughter* (1922).

A remarkable anonymous French postcard of 1925, taken in the Bois de Boulogne.

The gangster car as seen in *Million Dollar Haul* . . . and *Capone*.

In *The Singing Kid,* Al Jolson downs a city, which is knocked out. But the city would really die, if (below) the food lorries did not get through, as seen in *The Long Haul.*

vehicle of death and retribution and love. A whole generation of young Americans was meant to have been conceived in the back of model-T Fords. Cities choked and died, if the life-wheels of the automobiles and the lorries did not bring in the food and drink. The battered wrecks of the Detroit assembly lines were the last hope of the dirt-farmers

The explosives lorry plunges to its doom after it has saved the oil fire in Clouzot's *The Wages of Fear.*

An authentic picture of the original bandit Bonnie Parker, taken just before her death.

Faye Dunaway plays Bonnie to Warren Beatty's Clyde in Arthur Penn's movie.

Both the cops . . . and Bonnie die horribly by their cars.

of Oklahoma, making for California in *The Grapes of Wrath*, just as the thirties' roadsters were to be the vehicles of liberation for Arthur Penn's nostalgic recreation of the period, *Bonnie and Clyde*, where the rampaging four-wheeled big cars of past dream became the iron chargers of the bandits in love with freedom and in hate of the banks. In Corman's follow-up, *Big Bad Mama*, the old car is even more the burning chariot of fire. *(See Colour Section)*

Above: **The dream of speed in *Fast and Furious* (1927) . . . and (left) cabbie Cagney in *Taxi* (1932).**

Starring **ANN SHERIDAN PAT O'BRIEN**

As the cult of the car grew, so Hollywood moved in with the motor race movie. From such early racing attempts as *Fast and Furious* of 1927, and the films where Wallace Reid always played the racing demon, Warner Brothers began to use Cagney in the rough driver role, as a cabbie in *Taxi* and as a racing driver in Howard Hawks' production of *The Crowd Roars*, both made in 1932. In London, *The Times*, reviewing the second film, underscored the ambiguity of the genre. 'The various episodes of this romance of the American motor racing track are at least as painful as they are exciting . . . The ugly emotions of the crowd which delights in such disasters are represented with some accuracy, but it is not explained what we are to think of ourselves if we enjoy this film.' The two serious accidents and multitudinous skids of the tiny racers, all shot for realism

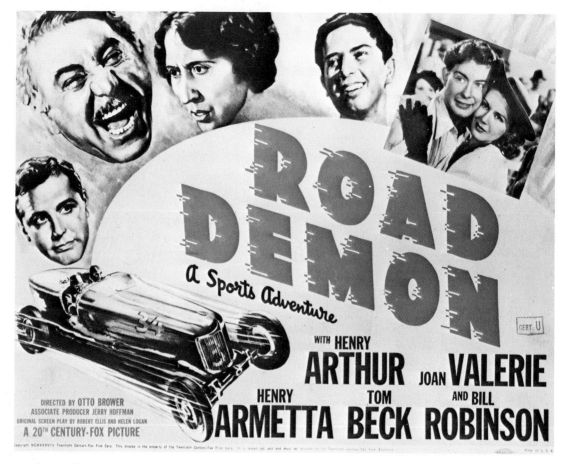

at the Indianapolis and Ventura and Ascot tracks, did give the film a crude excitement. Hawks shot so much racing footage that there was enough left in the vaults for a remake in 1939 called *Devil Wheels*.

There were other versions of the motor race. Some were small-scale, such as *Road Demon* and *Roadracers*. One MGM production of 1950, *To Please A Lady*, brought the aging Clark Gable in to play the Cagney role as a midget car racer on the Indianapolis Speedway; but it was not a great success. Not until Claude Lelouch's *A Man and a Woman* cast Jean-Louis Trintignant and Anouk Aimée in a racing drama did the big race spin off a film winner. And yet the film was a success more because of the strength of the love-story than because of the speed of the racing-cars. This was proved by the relative failure of the big racing pictures of the *macho* modern stars of the screen. Even Paul Newman could not make *Winning* into a success, despite stock footage of a

seventeen-car smash-up at Indianapolis. The same was true of both Frankenheimer's and Steve McQueen's efforts to do a genuine film about Grand Prix racing. The big cars were not enough – even with stars driving them – to fill the cinemas. Racing enthusiasts numbered only millions, and the speed-kings on their sleek wheels could not carry a movie. They had to be the subplot of a strong story.

Cars were better off as the instruments of menace in the thriller, the harpies rather than the demi-gods of the story. In the films of the great directors such as Godard or Hitchcock, the car has resonances beyond its appearance. It is fascism in *Made in U.S.A.*, it is conspiracy and disaster in *Pierrot le Fou*, it is the total savagery and inanity of bourgeois values in *Week-end*. For Hitchcock, the car can be both the vehicle of suspense and retribution. Who can ever forget the night-driving sequence in the rain in *Psycho* and the police car

The race from *Roadracers*.

From Lelouch's *A Man and a Woman*

Assassination by car in Godard's *Made in U.S.A.*

Car smash and car death in *Pierrot le Fou*.

Above: The famous traffic-jam in *Week-end*. *Below:* Car smash in *Week-end*.

The Minis cross the breakwater in *The Italian Job*.

stopping the girl with the stolen notes,
only to check her licence? Later, after the
terrible murder of the girl in the shower,
the slow sinking of the car in the swamp by
Anthony Perkins seems to be the destruction of all reason and evidence. Ingmar
Bergman, too, by the very quality of his
direction, can make even a Volkswagen
appear to be a deathwatch beetle in *Wild
Strawberries*. To the brilliant camera-eye, a
car is more than a car.

In the straight entertainment thriller,
however, the car is like a fairground whip
or dodg'em, cavorting and whisking and
leaping and crushing. The acrobatic Minis
in *The Italian Job* gave the film its international success. The flying cars on the hills
of San Francisco shot *Bullitt* up to the large
grosses. There was the extraordinary
sequence in *The Anderson Tapes* where the
getaway vans speed out of the removal van
and fail to break through the squad cars.
There is even the car as star in *Point Blank*
and *Vanishing Point,* where Barry Newman

drives and drives over the West, but must
finally meet his doom on the terminal road-
block of them all. Otherwise, spectacular
car chases and car crashes have become the
staple of nearly every thriller, from *McQ* to
Fear is the Key to a hundred other cops-and-
robbers escapades.

Rarely is the car now scripted into a film
as more than a spectacular turn of the wheel.
Occasionally an extraordinary film like
Duel emerges, where the contest between the
car and the heavy lorry is the guts of the
plot. The car was the supreme menace in
that underrated Mitchum thriller, *Cape Fear*.
It also is the conscious means of destroying
family and city in a host of films on urban
catastrophe, from the *Godfather* movies to
Fritz the Cat and *Day of the Locust* and *The
Cars That Ate Paris*. Even in cheap European
thrillers, designed for the male market, the
car has somehow become mixed up with
sex, so that it becomes the background for
the display of women, rather like a moving
shop window behind the female dummies

The cars leap . . . and smash in *Bullitt*.

Barry Newman's car finally meets its end in *Vanishing Point*.

John Wayne now needs a crashing car as a back-up in *McQ* – a long way from *Stagecoach*.

The chased car smashes through the garbage in *Fear is the Key*.

The child is menaced by the car driven by Mitchum in *Cape Fear*.

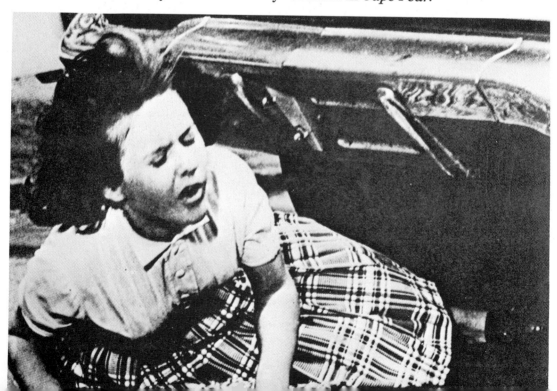

of the exploitation movie.

At the last resort, the automobile has never quite reached the heights of fantasy and dream where train smoke could raise us – and the rocket blast to come. It is a speedy, daring, lusty vehicle; but it invites the greed of possession, not the reverie of inaction. Only once in the post-war years did the incomparable Judy Holliday raise the modern chariot-on-wheels to a peak of avarice almost beyond the imagination of an oil-sheik. Then she rode off with her love at the finale in *The Solid Gold Cadillac*. Who can want more than *That*?

The cars are set alight in *Fritz the Cat*.

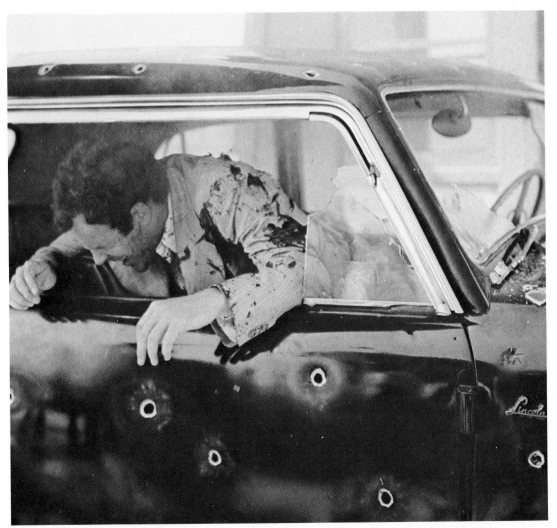

The hoodlum is riddled with bullets through the car body in *The Godfather*.

HUMAN GRACE, OUTER SPACE

Man's urge to reach the outer stars was first through the spirit, then through the body. The Ancient Greeks, of course, related the two. At Olympia and Delphi, gymnastics were religious; the speed and grace of the human body was a part of the worship of the gods. The shortage of oxygen in the lungs of the runners, the exertion of the leapers and wrestlers and discus-throwers, all produced a state of exaltation which was a physical kind of religous ecstasy. It took the Nazi director Leni Riefenstahl to reduce the Olympic Games to a sort of military ritual in her *Olympiad* of 1936. In fact, athletics are the way of transcending the human body, of escaping the limitations of the limbs.

Thus the fantasy of building some machine that will help us even more than a pole-vault to catapult us to the heavens. The space-rocket is the culmination of man's search for the ultimate. From the first telescope with its projectile shape probing to the far planets, men have wished to hurl their bodies to the moon as a first shot towards the ends of the universe. They have tried to put an explosive charge behind the church spire that has always pointed its finger towards the secrets of the heavens. In all the early space movies, the moon-rocket resembles a steeple shot from a gun – and indeed, the first actual Americans on the moon landed from what was originally little more than a spire-shaped giant rocket

Human beings are mere lines in Riefenstahl's *Olympiad* (1936).

In Méliès *A Trip to the Moon* of 1902, there is huge excitement in the Astronomic Club before the moonshot.

The shape of the spire and the planet at its simplest, representing man's aspirations at the New York World's Fair of 1939.

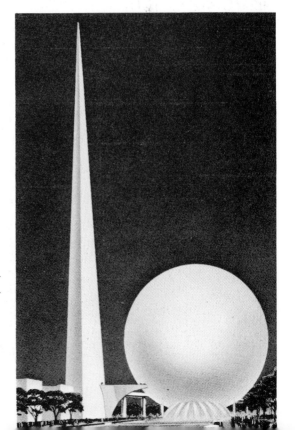

with sections of a metal steeple, which fell away in space.

Matching the crude ships-in-air of the early dreamers of spacecraft were the studio creations for the space-travellers of the early film serials. While the original dreamers put wings on their gods and sails on their airships, the makers of the space serials from *The Sky Splitter* of 1922 through *Flash Gordon* to the Buck Rogers strip in *Planet Outlaws* generally seemed to travel in hot-water tanks with amputated wings. Of course, as the moon-shots became more of a reality with the first successful German rocket-bombs, which landed on London in 1944, so the shape of the spaceships became more realistic and back to the general spire-

The moonshot takes place from a gigantic gun in H. G. Wells's *Things To Come* (1935).

In fantasy and reality, space-travel by rocket. These three stills come from *Missile Monsters* (below left), *Planet of the Apes* (above), and the Soviet documentary, *Blazing a Trail to the Stars* (below).

The winged Ancient Egyptian god Khensu . . . and the airship of the Jesuit de Lana of 1670.

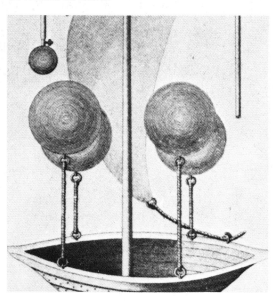

form. In *Rocketship X-M* and *First Man Into Space,* the spacecrafts were believable – as they certainly were in the documentary approach of the Gregory Peck vehicle, *Marooned.* When the technology of a landing on the moon was already known, fairly accurate versions of the later capsules and landing-craft could be constructed, as in *Moon Zero Two.*

In fantasy voyages, the old ideas of space *ships* survived, because their shapes were more traditional and mythological. In films

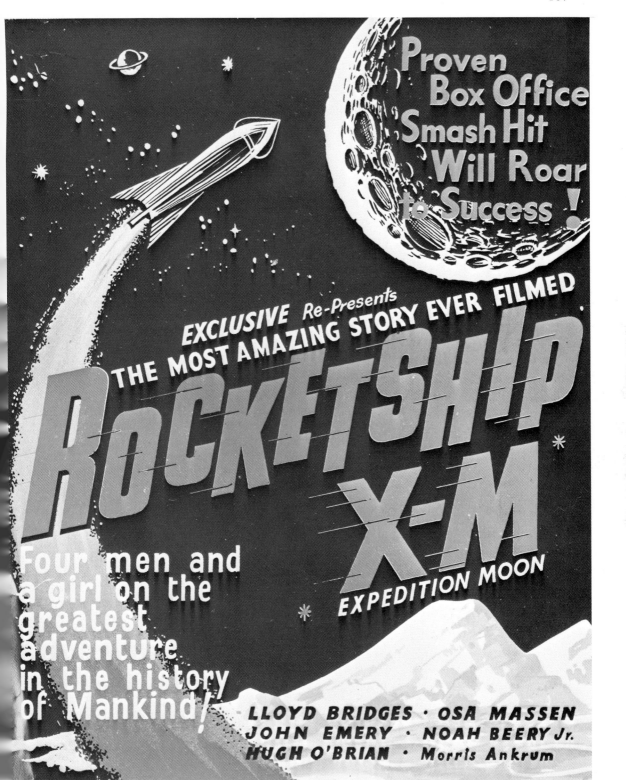

The moon landing-craft from *Moon Zero Two*. This film was rather upstaged by the actual landing of men on the moon, which anyone could see on television.

such as *Voyage to the End of the Universe* or in the excellent *Silent Running,* the space-ships were the heroes. They were definitely so in films that depended entirely on their special effects, such as *Thunderbirds Are Go,* which is based on the tricks of a successful children's television series. Particularly old-fashioned was the intravenous miniaturized sub-craft in *Fantastic Voyage,* which was injected into the bloodstream of an ill, important man to

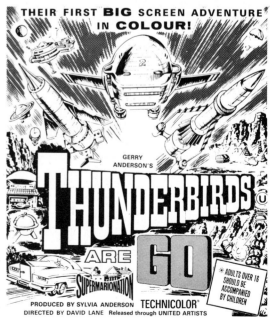

remove an obstruction in his heart. And as for the space technology of *Robinson Crusoe on Mars*, how could anyone ask for a more total confusion of the old ways and the new?

The space voyage, however, did produce its masterpiece like the battleship, the stagecoach, and the bicycle had already done. That was Stanley Kubrick's *2001*, which was fantasy and documentary, futurism and atavism. Beginning with ape-men and ending with a dream space-trip looking for the Word that was the Beginning, Kubrick's genius capped seven decades of directors' efforts to put on film the yearning desire of man in his effort to hurl his body to the most distant stars. We have reached the moon bodily and sent our craft to Mars. Our space probes travel nearly as far as our dreams through the expanding galaxy. We have escaped from earth and air into orbit and atmosphere. From the speed of the wheel, we search for the speed of light. Further. Further. Further . . .

In *Fantastic Voyage,* the miniature sub-craft is trapped by the nerves of the patient . . . and the tiny voyagers leave it to repair the patient's damaged heart.

Above and Right: By the wheel and the revolving drum, man becomes spaceman in Kubrick's *2001*. From the wheel as space-station, the rocket ship shoots to the limits of knowledge and the universe in *2001*.